THE BEST OF
HEATH ROBINSON

William Heath Robinson

THE
BEST OF
HEATH ROBINSON

W. Heath Robinson

Duckworth

First published in 1982 by
Gerald Duckworth & Co. Ltd.
The Old Piano Factory
43 Gloucester Crescent, London NW1.

ISBN 0 7156 1692 7 (cased)

Printed in Great Britain
by Unwin Brothers Limited
The Gresham Press, Old Woking, Surrey, England
A member of the Staples Printing Group

CONTENTS

INTRODUCTION

As Heath Robinson tells us in his autobiography *My Line of Life*, he was a great believer in the ordinary man, 'content to be ordinary: journeying along their way, these people are partners in the work of the greatest artists who have lived to proclaim the eternal beauty of the normal life of man. Even the humorous artist's part in this is not negligible. His humour can be human and full of charity; this last kind of humour may raise a laugh at the ordinary man, at his foibles and difficulties, but it is a brother's laugh in which he could join. Behind it all is a deep understanding of the part he plays and his courage in playing it.' It is this charity, on top of his superlative ingenuity, that animates the whole of Heath Robinson's work; it operates in every line of this anthology chosen from the ordinary man's daily adventures and predicaments, domestic, at work, at play, at war, and getting from place to place.

Sometimes, we are told, when he had completed a new drawing, he would summon members of his family into the studio and ask them if they could see 'how it works'. It made little difference if they couldn't: like all the greatest art, Heath Robinson's trembles on the brink of the impossible. Even his keenest fans cannot always agree about what is going on; and, as this assortment abundantly shows, some of his least easily explicable work is some of the most powerful.

M.H.

SOCIAL LIFE

Compact arrangement of the limited space in a
bungalow dining-room

Spring cleaning in Highgate Woods

Laying the Foundation Stone of the projected new structure to
replace Waterloo Bridge

The sunbathing wheel

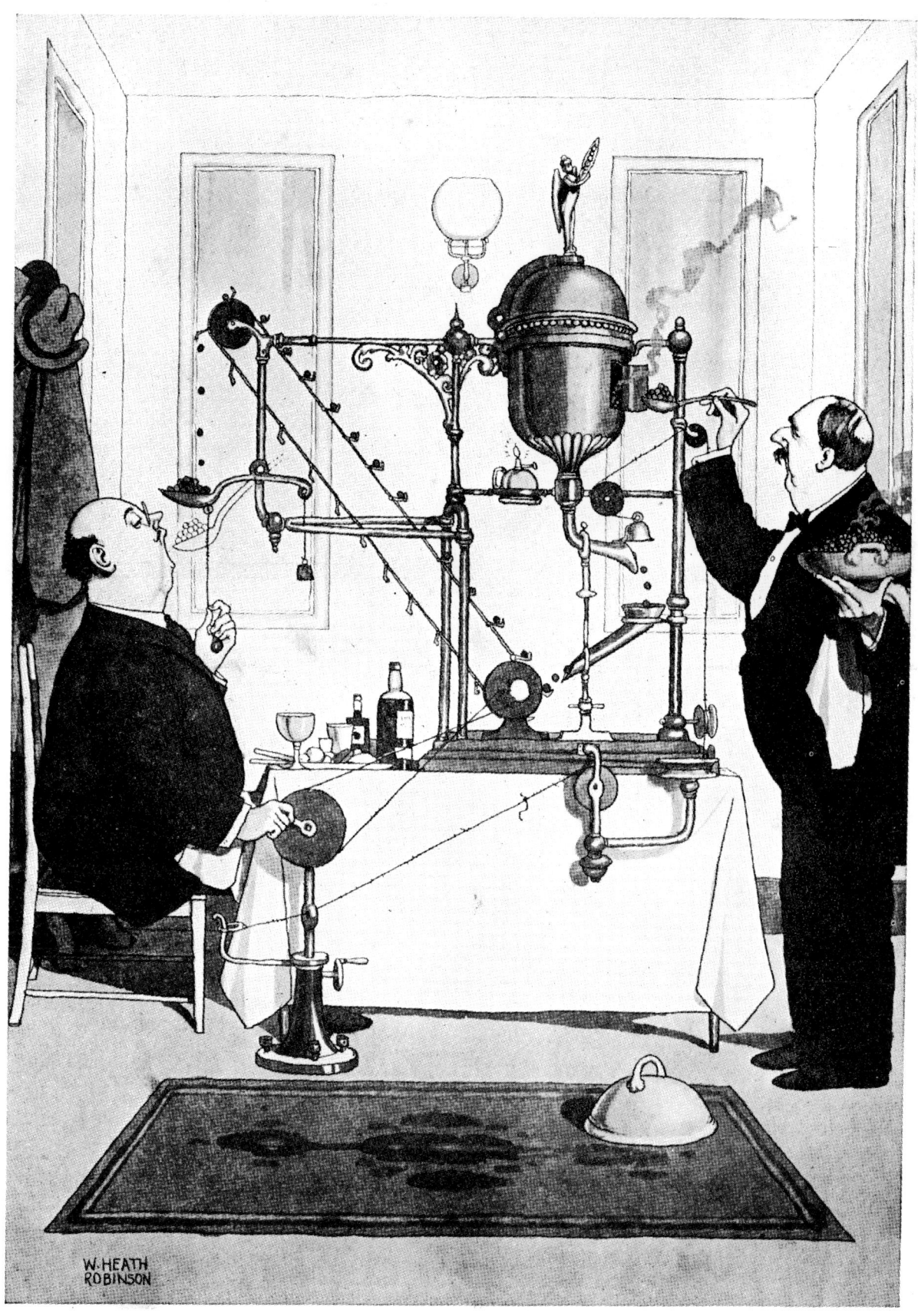

An interesting and elegant apparatus designed to overcome once for all the
difficulties of conveying green peas to the mouth

Flat life

The spare bedroom

Flat life
Sane economy of space at a wedding reception

Flat life

Some ingenious devices for use on chilly mornings

How to take advantage of the Savoy Orpheans dance music

Candidates for water divining

Plucky attempt to rescue a family overtaken by the tide

New top flat rescue apparatus

SPORT & PASTIMES

A new machine erected on Margate sands
for drying the hair after bathing

The Fall of Man

An intelligent green-keeper at 2.0 a.m., disguised as an early bird, scaring worms from a golfing green

How coal was first discovered in Scotland

The St. Andrew's bunker chair, designed to relieve golfers of the necessity of walking round bunkers

The new golf car for the comfort of golfers

The origin of plus fours

The discovery of the principle of the parachute during a landslip in
the Apennines

The hydro-multi-aeroplane

Double cross tennis

For economising space in local tournaments and generally gingering up the game

Multi-tennis

For the convenience of bathers in rough weather

Swimming the Channel
Some simple devices to ensure success

Toeing for crabs at Herne Bay

Clam spearing

Widgeon bluffing on the Roaring Fork

Catching young tarpon

Trapping the polecat

INDUSTRY

Testing the waterproof qualities of umbrellas
in an up-to-date brolley works

A patent double-action grinder for mashing asbestos fibre

Testing golf drivers

Stretching spaghetti

Square pegs into round holes

Egg armour plating

Testing artificial teeth

Doubling Gloucester cheeses

One of the old machines for counting and checking peas after haulage

Squaring the "Johnnie Walker" bottles

An old and somewhat laborious method of refrigerating a fresh herring

A dream of the future

Sectional view of old fashioned manhandled warehouse with stories

The new patent air brush in use in the studio preparing a drawing
for reproduction

The latest machinery for the mass production of horseshoes

Interesting treatment of cattle on an Argentine stock farm to make the meat tender and soft before killing

Cultivating buoyancy, toughness and resisting power in hides for footballs
in the stockyards of a football factory

Anti-litter machine

GETTING FROM A TO B

Celebrating the payment of the last instalment

The puncture

Noah and the Flood

Building the first locomotive

Boring the first tunnel with an early type of rotary excavator

The new humane cow-catcher

Mr. W. Heath Robinson's own private railway engine, not often allowed on the G.W.R.

The first excursion train

Relieving the tedium of waiting for the signal on the slow train—
between Paddington and Land's End via Southampton, Hereford and
Weston-Super-Mare

The last post for the country—an early attempt at picking up mails
without stopping

An antiquated method of filling the boilers without stopping the engine
before the introduction of the water-trough system

Goods and passengers carried together in the open

The building of Saltash Bridge

One of the many suggestions for doing without tunnels

Sectional view of the excavations for the Severn Tunnel, showing the hard and fossiliferous nature of the ground to be penetrated

How they train railway porters to manœuvre their loads on crowded
platforms

Installing the electric telegraph between Paddington and Slough

A very early type of mechanical signal, now rarely to be seen!

W. HEATH ROBINSON

A new snow-plough for clearing a footpath after a heavy fall

A leak in the Channel Tunnel

WAR

Divided counsels

The fortune of war

The bit that kept up

Helping a bird to
build its nest

Washing day in the
German Army

Home thoughts. Tommy (confused by the sudden encounter): "Er—
er—third return to 'Ammersmith!"

Nach Paris!   First lessons in the goose-step

Hague Convention defied! Lachrymosing the British by onion-whittling
under cover of night

Neutral!   A Swiss shepherd watching a battle on the frontier

The Boche-catcher

British patent (applied for).   The lancing wheel for teaching young lancers
to lance

Camouflage on Salisbury Plain

For the War Inventions Board.   The Pilsner pump for tapping the enemy's
supper beer

The trench-sealer

Hit or Missler gun

OH U!   The German periscoper: "Ach Himmel! Dot most be der Peautiful
Ben Nevis of vich ve 'ave 'eard so mooch!"

The Subzeppmarinellin

Wangling war films.   How to make and fake them: The popular film of a
Taube soaring over Rheims Cathedral

Spiked!   Unfortunate mishap to a Zeppelin through a lack of proper caution
in descending

The shelter

For the War Inventions Board. The blow-bomb for extinguishing the fuses
of Zeppelin bombs

Deceiving Nazi dive-bombers

The multi-movement bomb-catcher

A matter of time